50 Elegant Appetizer Recipes for Home

By: Kelly Johnson

Table of Contents

- Prosciutto-Wrapped Asparagus
- Smoked Salmon Crostini
- Stuffed Mushrooms with Creamy Spinach
- Caprese Skewers with Balsamic Glaze
- Mini Lobster Tarts
- Bacon-Wrapped Dates with Goat Cheese
- Cucumber Cups with Dill Cream Cheese
- Shrimp Cocktail with Tangy Cocktail Sauce
- Brie and Raspberry Phyllo Cups
- Truffle Deviled Eggs
- Pesto and Sundried Tomato Pinwheels
- Fig and Prosciutto Bruschetta
- Blue Cheese-Stuffed Olives
- Crab and Avocado Salad Spoons
- Mini Quiches with Gruyere and Herbs
- Teriyaki Chicken Skewers
- Grilled Vegetable Antipasto Platter
- Cherry Tomato and Mozzarella Bites
- Spinach and Artichoke Stuffed Mini Peppers
- Seared Scallops with Lemon Butter
- Apricot and Brie Puff Pastry Bites
- Garlic and Herb Marinated Feta Cubes
- Chicken Satay with Peanut Dipping Sauce
- Pomegranate and Goat Cheese Crostini
- Olive Tapenade on Crostini
- Gourmet Deviled Quail Eggs
- Rosemary and Sea Salt Marcona Almonds
- Pear and Blue Cheese Tartlets
- Gruyere and Caramelized Onion Puffs
- Tuna Tartare with Avocado
- Herbed Goat Cheese-Stuffed Cherry Tomatoes
- Lobster Salad in Endive Spears
- Honey Sriracha Glazed Meatballs
- Roasted Red Pepper Hummus Cups
- Coconut Shrimp with Mango Salsa

- Pistachio and Cranberry Goat Cheese Balls
- White Truffle and Parmesan Popcorn
- Sherry-infused Mushroom Crostini
- Spicy Tuna Rolls in Cucumber Cups
- Watermelon Feta Mint Skewers
- Saffron and Lemon Risotto Balls
- Roquefort and Walnut Stuffed Figs
- Basil Pesto Palmiers
- Roasted Beet and Whipped Goat Cheese Crostini
- Chicken Liver Pate on Baguette Slices
- Sushi-grade Tuna Nachos
- Raspberry and Brie Puff Pastry Pinwheels
- Marinated Artichoke Hearts with Parmesan
- Mini Crab Cakes with Remoulade Sauce
- Blue Cheese and Walnut-Stuffed Dates

Prosciutto-Wrapped Asparagus

Ingredients:

- 1 bunch of fresh asparagus spears (about 1 pound)
- 10-12 slices of prosciutto
- Olive oil
- Black pepper, freshly ground
- Balsamic glaze (optional, for drizzling)

Instructions:

Preheat the Oven:

Preheat your oven to 400°F (200°C).

Prepare Asparagus:

Trim the tough ends from the asparagus spears. If they are thick, you can peel the bottom part of the asparagus to ensure tenderness.

Wrap with Prosciutto:

Take a slice of prosciutto and wrap it around each asparagus spear, starting at the bottom and spiraling up towards the tip. Repeat for all asparagus spears.

Arrange on Baking Sheet:

Place the prosciutto-wrapped asparagus on a baking sheet lined with parchment paper, making sure they are not too crowded.

Drizzle with Olive Oil:

Lightly drizzle the wrapped asparagus with olive oil, ensuring they are evenly coated.

Season with Pepper:

Sprinkle freshly ground black pepper over the asparagus for added flavor.

Bake:

Bake in the preheated oven for about 10-15 minutes or until the prosciutto is crispy and the asparagus is tender but still has a slight crunch.

Serve:

Once done, remove from the oven and transfer the prosciutto-wrapped asparagus to a serving platter. Optionally, drizzle with balsamic glaze for extra flavor.

Enjoy:

Serve the Prosciutto-Wrapped Asparagus as a delightful appetizer or side dish. They can be enjoyed warm or at room temperature.

This dish is not only elegant but also a delicious combination of the salty prosciutto and the fresh, slightly sweet flavor of asparagus. It's perfect for gatherings or as a starter for a special meal.

Smoked Salmon Crostini

Ingredients:

- Baguette or French bread, thinly sliced
- 8 ounces (about 225g) smoked salmon
- 1/2 cup cream cheese, softened
- 1/4 cup sour cream
- 1 tablespoon fresh dill, chopped
- 1 tablespoon capers, drained
- 1 small red onion, thinly sliced
- Lemon wedges for garnish
- Freshly ground black pepper

Instructions:

Preheat the Oven:

Preheat your oven to 375°F (190°C).

Slice the Baguette:

Slice the baguette or French bread into thin rounds. Place the slices on a baking sheet.

Toast the Bread:

Toast the bread slices in the preheated oven for about 5-7 minutes or until they are golden and crisp. Keep an eye on them to avoid burning.

Prepare Cream Cheese Mixture:

In a bowl, combine the softened cream cheese and sour cream. Mix until smooth and well combined.

Add Dill:

Stir in the chopped fresh dill into the cream cheese mixture. This adds a burst of fresh flavor.

Assemble Crostini:

Spread a thin layer of the cream cheese mixture onto each toasted bread slice.

Top with Smoked Salmon:

Place a piece of smoked salmon on top of each crostini. You can fold or arrange it in a decorative way.

Garnish:

Sprinkle capers over the smoked salmon. Add a few slices of red onion on top for a bit of crunch.

Season and Garnish:

Season the crostini with freshly ground black pepper. Garnish with additional dill and lemon wedges.

Serve:

Arrange the Smoked Salmon Crostini on a serving platter and serve immediately.

Enjoy:

These crostini can be enjoyed as a sophisticated appetizer or as part of a larger spread. The combination of smoked salmon, creamy cheese, and fresh herbs creates a delightful flavor profile.

Smoked Salmon Crostini is not only delicious but also visually appealing, making it an excellent choice for entertaining guests or simply enjoying a special moment.

Stuffed Mushrooms with Creamy Spinach

Ingredients:

- 12 large mushrooms, cleaned and stems removed
- 1 tablespoon olive oil
- 1 small onion, finely chopped
- 2 cloves garlic, minced
- 4 cups fresh spinach, chopped
- 1/2 cup cream cheese
- 1/4 cup grated Parmesan cheese
- Salt and pepper to taste
- 1/2 cup breadcrumbs (optional, for topping)
- Fresh parsley, chopped (for garnish)

Instructions:

Preheat the oven to 375°F (190°C).
Heat olive oil in a skillet over medium heat. Add chopped onion and cook until softened, about 3-4 minutes.
Add minced garlic and cook for an additional 1-2 minutes until fragrant.
Add chopped spinach to the skillet and cook until wilted, stirring occasionally.
Stir in the cream cheese and Parmesan cheese, allowing them to melt and create a creamy mixture. Season with salt and pepper to taste.
Remove the skillet from heat and let the mixture cool slightly.
While the mixture is cooling, lightly grease a baking dish. Place the cleaned mushrooms in the dish, cavity side up.
Spoon the creamy spinach mixture into each mushroom cavity, pressing it down gently.
If desired, sprinkle breadcrumbs over the top of each stuffed mushroom for added crunch.
Bake in the preheated oven for about 15-20 minutes or until the mushrooms are tender and the tops are golden brown.
Garnish with chopped fresh parsley before serving.

These stuffed mushrooms with creamy spinach are a delightful combination of earthy mushrooms and rich, flavorful spinach. Enjoy them as a tasty appetizer or a side dish for your next meal!

Caprese Skewers with Balsamic Glaze

Ingredients:

- Fresh mozzarella balls (ciliegine or small mozzarella pearls)
- Cherry tomatoes
- Fresh basil leaves
- Balsamic glaze
- Extra virgin olive oil
- Salt and pepper to taste
- Wooden skewers

Instructions:

Prepare Ingredients:
- If you're using large mozzarella balls, cut them into bite-sized pieces.
- Wash and dry the cherry tomatoes.
- Pick fresh basil leaves.

Assemble Skewers:
- Take a wooden skewer and thread on a mozzarella ball, followed by a folded basil leaf and a cherry tomato.
- Repeat the pattern until the skewer is filled, leaving a bit of space at the ends for easy handling.

Arrange on Serving Platter:
- Arrange the assembled Caprese skewers on a serving platter.

Drizzle with Olive Oil:
- Drizzle extra virgin olive oil over the skewers. This adds a nice richness to the dish.

Season with Salt and Pepper:
- Sprinkle a bit of salt and pepper over the skewers. Adjust according to your taste.

Balsamic Glaze:
- Drizzle balsamic glaze over the skewers. This provides a sweet and tangy flavor that complements the other ingredients.

Serve:
- Serve the Caprese skewers immediately, or you can refrigerate them for a short time before serving.

Garnish (Optional):

- Optionally, you can garnish with additional fresh basil leaves or a sprinkle of dried oregano for extra flavor.

These Caprese skewers with balsamic glaze make a delightful and visually appealing appetizer, perfect for gatherings, parties, or as a light starter to a meal. Enjoy!

Mini Lobster Tarts

Ingredients:

For the Tart Shells:

- 1 1/2 cups all-purpose flour
- 1/2 cup unsalted butter, cold and cut into small cubes
- 1/4 teaspoon salt
- 3-4 tablespoons ice water

For the Lobster Filling:

- 1 cup cooked lobster meat, chopped into small pieces
- 1/4 cup mayonnaise
- 2 tablespoons Greek yogurt or sour cream
- 1 tablespoon fresh chives, finely chopped
- 1 teaspoon Dijon mustard
- Salt and pepper to taste

For Garnish:

- Fresh chives, chopped
- Lemon wedges

Instructions:

For the Tart Shells:

In a food processor, combine the flour, cold butter, and salt. Pulse until the mixture resembles coarse crumbs.
Add ice water, one tablespoon at a time, and pulse until the dough starts to come together. Be careful not to overmix.
Turn the dough out onto a lightly floured surface and knead it just until it forms a ball. Wrap the dough in plastic wrap and refrigerate for at least 30 minutes.
Preheat your oven to 375°F (190°C).

Roll out the chilled dough on a floured surface to about 1/8-inch thickness. Cut out rounds using a small cookie cutter or the rim of a glass.

Press the rounds into mini tart pans or mini muffin tins. Prick the bottoms with a fork to prevent them from puffing up during baking.

Bake the tart shells for 12-15 minutes or until golden brown. Allow them to cool completely before filling.

For the Lobster Filling:

In a bowl, mix together the chopped lobster meat, mayonnaise, Greek yogurt (or sour cream), chives, Dijon mustard, salt, and pepper. Adjust seasoning to taste.

Spoon the lobster mixture into the cooled tart shells.

For Garnish:

Garnish each mini lobster tart with a sprinkle of chopped fresh chives.

Serve the mini lobster tarts with lemon wedges on the side.

These mini lobster tarts are perfect for special occasions or as an elegant appetizer for a dinner party. Enjoy!

Bacon-Wrapped Dates with Goat Cheese

Ingredients:

For the Tart Shells:

- 1 1/2 cups all-purpose flour
- 1/2 cup unsalted butter, cold and cut into small cubes
- 1/4 teaspoon salt
- 3-4 tablespoons ice water

For the Lobster Filling:

- 1 cup cooked lobster meat, chopped into small pieces
- 1/4 cup mayonnaise
- 2 tablespoons Greek yogurt or sour cream
- 1 tablespoon fresh chives, finely chopped
- 1 teaspoon Dijon mustard
- Salt and pepper to taste

For Garnish:

- Fresh chives, chopped
- Lemon wedges

Instructions:

For the Tart Shells:

> In a food processor, combine the flour, cold butter, and salt. Pulse until the mixture resembles coarse crumbs.
> Add ice water, one tablespoon at a time, and pulse until the dough starts to come together. Be careful not to overmix.
> Turn the dough out onto a lightly floured surface and knead it just until it forms a ball. Wrap the dough in plastic wrap and refrigerate for at least 30 minutes.
> Preheat your oven to 375°F (190°C).

Roll out the chilled dough on a floured surface to about 1/8-inch thickness. Cut out rounds using a small cookie cutter or the rim of a glass.

Press the rounds into mini tart pans or mini muffin tins. Prick the bottoms with a fork to prevent them from puffing up during baking.

Bake the tart shells for 12-15 minutes or until golden brown. Allow them to cool completely before filling.

For the Lobster Filling:

In a bowl, mix together the chopped lobster meat, mayonnaise, Greek yogurt (or sour cream), chives, Dijon mustard, salt, and pepper. Adjust seasoning to taste.

Spoon the lobster mixture into the cooled tart shells.

For Garnish:

Garnish each mini lobster tart with a sprinkle of chopped fresh chives.

Serve the mini lobster tarts with lemon wedges on the side.

These mini lobster tarts are perfect for special occasions or as an elegant appetizer for a dinner party. Enjoy!

Cucumber Cups with Dill Cream Cheese

Ingredients:

- 2 large English cucumbers
- 8 oz (225g) cream cheese, softened
- 2 tablespoons fresh dill, chopped
- 1 tablespoon fresh chives, chopped
- 1 clove garlic, minced
- Salt and pepper to taste
- Optional: Smoked salmon or small shrimp for topping
- Optional: Lemon zest for garnish

Instructions:

Prepare the Cucumbers:
- Wash the cucumbers thoroughly. Cut off the ends and slice them into 1 to 1.5-inch rounds.

Scoop Out the Center:
- Use a small spoon or a melon baller to gently scoop out the center of each cucumber round, creating a cup. Be careful not to scoop through the bottom.

Prepare the Dill Cream Cheese:
- In a bowl, combine the softened cream cheese, chopped fresh dill, chopped chives, minced garlic, salt, and pepper. Mix well until all ingredients are incorporated.

Fill the Cucumber Cups:
- Spoon or pipe the dill cream cheese mixture into each cucumber cup, filling them to the top.

Optional Toppings:
- If desired, top each cucumber cup with a small piece of smoked salmon or a cooked shrimp.

Garnish:
- Garnish the cucumber cups with additional chopped dill or a sprinkle of lemon zest for a burst of freshness.

Chill:
- Refrigerate the cucumber cups for at least 30 minutes before serving to allow the flavors to meld.

Serve:
- Arrange the cucumber cups on a serving platter and serve them chilled.

These cucumber cups with dill cream cheese are not only visually appealing but also a delicious and healthy appetizer option. They are perfect for summer gatherings or any event where you want to offer a light and refreshing dish. Enjoy!

Shrimp Cocktail with Tangy Cocktail Sauce

Ingredients:

For the Shrimp:

- 1 pound large shrimp, peeled and deveined
- 1 tablespoon olive oil
- Salt and pepper to taste
- Lemon wedges for garnish

For the Cocktail Sauce:

- 1 cup ketchup
- 2 tablespoons prepared horseradish
- 1 tablespoon Worcestershire sauce
- 1 tablespoon fresh lemon juice
- 1 teaspoon hot sauce (adjust to taste)
- Salt and pepper to taste

Instructions:

For the Shrimp:

Prepare the Shrimp: Preheat a large skillet over medium-high heat. Toss the shrimp with olive oil, salt, and pepper.
Cook the Shrimp: Cook the shrimp in the preheated skillet for 2-3 minutes per side or until they turn pink and opaque. Be careful not to overcook them. Remove from heat and let them cool.
Chill the Shrimp: Once the shrimp are cooked and cooled, refrigerate them for at least 30 minutes before serving.
For the Cocktail Sauce:
Mix the Ingredients: In a bowl, combine the ketchup, prepared horseradish, Worcestershire sauce, fresh lemon juice, hot sauce, salt, and pepper. Stir well to combine.
Chill the Sauce: Refrigerate the cocktail sauce for at least 30 minutes to allow the flavors to meld.

Serve:
Arrange the Shrimp: Arrange the chilled shrimp on a serving platter or individual cocktail glasses.
Serve with Sauce: Serve the shrimp with the tangy cocktail sauce on the side.
Garnish: Garnish with lemon wedges for a fresh burst of citrus flavor.
Optional Presentation: For an elegant presentation, you can place some ice in a serving dish and arrange the shrimp around it to keep them chilled.

This shrimp cocktail with tangy cocktail sauce is perfect for any occasion, whether it's a casual gathering or a formal dinner party. It's a classic appetizer that never goes out of style. Enjoy!

Brie and Raspberry Phyllo Cups

Ingredients:

- 1 package (15 count) mini phyllo cups (pre-baked)
- 6 oz (about 170g) Brie cheese, rind removed and cut into small cubes
- 1/2 cup raspberry preserves
- Fresh mint leaves for garnish (optional)

Instructions:

Preheat Oven:
- If your phyllo cups are not pre-baked, follow the package instructions for baking. If they are pre-baked, there's no need to preheat the oven.

Prepare Brie:
- Remove the rind from the Brie cheese and cut it into small cubes.

Fill Phyllo Cups:
- Place the pre-baked phyllo cups on a serving platter or a baking sheet.
- Add a cube of Brie cheese into each phyllo cup.

Add Raspberry Preserves:
- Spoon a small amount of raspberry preserves over the Brie in each cup. You can adjust the amount based on your preference for sweetness.

Optional Baking (if desired):
- If you'd like to serve the cups warm, you can bake them in a preheated oven at 350°F (175°C) for about 5-7 minutes, just until the Brie starts to melt.

Garnish:
- Garnish each Brie and raspberry phyllo cup with a small mint leaf for a fresh touch.

Serve:
- Arrange the cups on a serving platter and serve immediately.

These Brie and raspberry phyllo cups are not only delicious but also visually appealing, making them a perfect appetizer for parties, brunches, or any special occasion. The combination of creamy Brie and sweet raspberry preserves creates a delightful flavor contrast in each bite. Enjoy!

Truffle Deviled Eggs

Ingredients:

- 6 large eggs
- 2 tablespoons mayonnaise
- 1 teaspoon Dijon mustard
- 1 teaspoon truffle oil
- Salt and pepper to taste
- Chives or fresh parsley for garnish
- Truffle salt (optional, for extra truffle flavor)

Instructions:

Boil the Eggs:
- Place the eggs in a saucepan and cover them with water.
- Bring the water to a boil, then reduce the heat to a simmer and cook for about 10-12 minutes.
- Once cooked, transfer the eggs to a bowl of ice water to cool before peeling.

Peel and Cut Eggs:
- Peel the cooled hard-boiled eggs and cut them in half lengthwise.
- Carefully remove the yolks and place them in a separate bowl.

Prepare the Filling:
- Mash the egg yolks with a fork or a potato masher until they are finely crumbled.

Add Ingredients:
- Add mayonnaise, Dijon mustard, truffle oil, salt, and pepper to the mashed yolks. Mix until well combined.

Fill the Egg Whites:
- Spoon or pipe the truffle-flavored yolk mixture back into the egg white halves.

Garnish:
- Garnish each deviled egg with finely chopped chives or fresh parsley.

Optional Truffle Salt:
- For an extra layer of truffle flavor, sprinkle a tiny amount of truffle salt over the deviled eggs.

Chill and Serve:

- Refrigerate the truffle deviled eggs for at least 30 minutes before serving to allow the flavors to meld.

Serve:
- Arrange the deviled eggs on a serving platter and serve them chilled.

These truffle deviled eggs are an elegant appetizer, perfect for upscale gatherings or as a unique addition to any party spread. The truffle oil adds a luxurious touch, making these deviled eggs stand out with rich and aromatic flavors. Enjoy!

Pesto and Sundried Tomato Pinwheels

Ingredients:

- 1 sheet of puff pastry, thawed if frozen
- 1/4 cup pesto sauce (store-bought or homemade)
- 1/4 cup sundried tomatoes, chopped
- 1/3 cup shredded mozzarella cheese
- 1 tablespoon grated Parmesan cheese
- Fresh basil leaves for garnish (optional)

Instructions:

Preheat Oven:
- Preheat your oven to the temperature specified on the puff pastry package (usually around 375°F or 190°C).

Roll Out Puff Pastry:
- Roll out the puff pastry sheet on a lightly floured surface to smooth out any creases.

Spread Pesto:
- Spread an even layer of pesto over the entire surface of the puff pastry.

Add Sundried Tomatoes:
- Sprinkle the chopped sundried tomatoes evenly over the pesto.

Sprinkle Cheese:
- Sprinkle the shredded mozzarella and grated Parmesan cheese over the pesto and sundried tomatoes.

Roll the Puff Pastry:
- Starting from one edge, carefully roll the puff pastry sheet into a log or cylinder. Roll it tightly to ensure the pinwheels hold their shape.

Chill (Optional):
- If time allows, you can refrigerate the rolled puff pastry for about 15-20 minutes. This makes it easier to slice.

Slice Into Pinwheels:
- Using a sharp knife, slice the rolled puff pastry into 1/2-inch to 1-inch thick pinwheels.

Bake:
- Place the pinwheels on a baking sheet lined with parchment paper.
- Bake in the preheated oven for 12-15 minutes or until the pinwheels are golden brown and puffed up.

Garnish:
- If desired, garnish the pinwheels with fresh basil leaves or additional grated Parmesan after baking.

Serve:
- Allow the pinwheels to cool slightly before serving. They can be served warm or at room temperature.

These pesto and sundried tomato pinwheels are a flavorful and easy-to-make appetizer that's sure to be a hit at any event. They combine the richness of pesto, the sweetness of sundried tomatoes, and the gooeyness of melted cheese in a delightful bite-sized treat. Enjoy!

Fig and Prosciutto Bruschetta

Ingredients:

- Baguette or French bread, sliced
- Fresh figs, sliced
- Prosciutto slices
- Goat cheese or blue cheese, crumbled
- Honey, for drizzling
- Balsamic glaze, for drizzling
- Fresh basil leaves, for garnish (optional)

Instructions:

Preheat Oven:
- Preheat your oven to 375°F (190°C).

Toast the Bread:
- Arrange the bread slices on a baking sheet and toast them in the preheated oven until they are lightly golden and crisp. This usually takes about 5-7 minutes, but keep an eye on them to prevent burning.

Assemble Bruschetta:
- Once the bread is toasted, let it cool slightly. Then, spread a layer of goat cheese or blue cheese on each slice.

Add Prosciutto and Figs:
- Top each bread slice with a slice of prosciutto, folded or draped to fit nicely.
- Place a few slices of fresh fig on top of the prosciutto.

Drizzle with Honey and Balsamic Glaze:
- Drizzle honey and balsamic glaze over each bruschetta. The sweetness of honey complements the figs, and balsamic glaze adds a tangy touch.

Garnish:
- If desired, garnish each bruschetta with fresh basil leaves for a pop of color and additional flavor.

Serve:
- Arrange the fig and prosciutto bruschetta on a serving platter and serve immediately.

This fig and prosciutto bruschetta offers a delightful combination of sweet, savory, and tangy flavors. It's a perfect appetizer for a sophisticated gathering or a special occasion. The contrast of textures and flavors makes it a crowd-pleaser. Enjoy!

Blue Cheese-Stuffed Olives

Ingredients:

- Large green olives (with pits or pitted)
- Blue cheese (choose a variety you enjoy)
- Extra virgin olive oil (optional)
- Fresh herbs like thyme or rosemary (optional, for garnish)

Instructions:

Prepare Olives:
- If the olives have pits, carefully make a lengthwise slit in each olive using a small knife. If using pitted olives, you can create a small cavity by gently pressing on each olive.

Stuff with Blue Cheese:
- Take small pieces of blue cheese and stuff them into the cavities of the olives. Use your fingers or a small spoon to press the cheese into the olives.

Optional: Drizzle with Olive Oil:
- If desired, drizzle a bit of extra virgin olive oil over the stuffed olives. This adds an extra layer of richness to the flavor.

Optional: Garnish with Fresh Herbs:
- Garnish the blue cheese-stuffed olives with fresh herbs like thyme or rosemary for a pop of color and added freshness.

Serve:
- Arrange the stuffed olives on a serving plate or in a bowl.

Chill (Optional):
- If time allows, you can refrigerate the stuffed olives for about 30 minutes to allow the flavors to meld.

Serve:
- Serve the blue cheese-stuffed olives at room temperature or slightly chilled.

These blue cheese-stuffed olives make for a delicious and sophisticated appetizer. They are perfect for cocktail parties, wine tastings, or as part of a charcuterie board. The salty brininess of the olives combined with the creamy and tangy blue cheese creates a delightful burst of flavor. Enjoy!

Crab and Avocado Salad Spoons

Ingredients:

- 1 cup lump crab meat, cooked and picked through for shells
- 1 ripe avocado, diced
- 1/4 cup red onion, finely chopped
- 1/4 cup cucumber, finely diced
- 2 tablespoons fresh cilantro or parsley, chopped
- 1 tablespoon mayonnaise
- 1 tablespoon sour cream or Greek yogurt
- 1 tablespoon fresh lime juice
- Salt and pepper to taste
- Mini salad spoons or endive leaves for serving

Instructions:

Prepare Crab Meat:
- Ensure that the crab meat is picked through for any shells.

Make the Salad:
- In a mixing bowl, combine the lump crab meat, diced avocado, chopped red onion, diced cucumber, and chopped cilantro or parsley.

Prepare Dressing:
- In a small bowl, whisk together mayonnaise, sour cream or Greek yogurt, fresh lime juice, salt, and pepper.

Combine Salad and Dressing:
- Pour the dressing over the crab and avocado mixture. Gently toss until all ingredients are well coated.

Adjust Seasoning:
- Taste the salad and adjust the seasoning if needed with more salt, pepper, or lime juice.

Chill (Optional):
- If time allows, refrigerate the crab and avocado salad for about 30 minutes to allow the flavors to meld.

Serve in Spoons or Endive Leaves:
- Spoon the crab and avocado salad onto mini salad spoons or arrange them in endive leaves for a stylish presentation.

Garnish (Optional):

- Garnish with additional chopped cilantro or parsley for a fresh touch.

Serve:
- Serve the crab and avocado salad spoons immediately, offering a refreshing and flavorful appetizer.

These crab and avocado salad spoons are not only delicious but also make for a beautiful and easy-to-eat presentation. The combination of sweet crab meat, creamy avocado, and zesty dressing creates a delightful bite-sized treat. Enjoy!

Mini Quiches with Gruyere and Herbs

Ingredients:

For the Quiche Filling:

- 4 large eggs
- 1 cup heavy cream or half-and-half
- 1 cup Gruyere cheese, shredded
- 2 tablespoons fresh chives, chopped
- 1 tablespoon fresh parsley, chopped
- Salt and pepper to taste

For the Quiche Crust:

- 1 package of pre-made mini tart shells or phyllo cups (or make your own crust if you prefer)

Instructions:

Preheat Oven:
- Preheat your oven to 375°F (190°C).

Prepare Tart Shells:
- If you are using pre-made mini tart shells or phyllo cups, arrange them on a baking sheet. If making your own crust, follow the crust recipe and press it into mini tart pans.

Make the Quiche Filling:
- In a bowl, whisk together eggs, heavy cream or half-and-half, shredded Gruyere, chopped chives, chopped parsley, salt, and pepper. Mix until well combined.

Fill the Tart Shells:
- Spoon or pour the quiche filling into each tart shell, leaving a little space at the top for the quiches to puff up as they bake.

Bake:
- Bake in the preheated oven for about 15-20 minutes or until the quiches are set and the tops are golden brown.

Cool:
- Allow the mini quiches to cool for a few minutes before serving.

Garnish (Optional):

- Garnish each mini quiche with additional chopped herbs for a fresh touch.

Serve:
- Arrange the mini quiches on a serving platter and serve them warm or at room temperature.

These mini quiches with Gruyere and herbs are a delicious and versatile appetizer. The creamy texture of Gruyere, paired with the freshness of herbs, creates a delightful flavor in each bite-sized quiche. Enjoy!

Teriyaki Chicken Skewers

Ingredients:

For the Teriyaki Marinade:

- 1/2 cup soy sauce
- 1/4 cup mirin (Japanese sweet rice wine)
- 2 tablespoons sake or dry white wine
- 2 tablespoons brown sugar
- 2 cloves garlic, minced
- 1 teaspoon fresh ginger, grated
- 1 tablespoon cornstarch (optional, for thickening)

For the Chicken Skewers:

- 1.5 pounds boneless, skinless chicken thighs or breasts, cut into bite-sized pieces
- Wooden or metal skewers
- Sesame seeds and chopped green onions for garnish (optional)
- Cooking oil for grilling or pan-searing

Instructions:

Prepare Marinade:
- In a bowl, whisk together soy sauce, mirin, sake or white wine, brown sugar, minced garlic, and grated ginger. If you prefer a thicker sauce, mix in the cornstarch until well combined.

Marinate Chicken:
- Place the chicken pieces in a shallow dish or a zip-top bag. Pour about half of the teriyaki marinade over the chicken, reserving the rest for basting and serving. Marinate the chicken in the refrigerator for at least 30 minutes or ideally a few hours for better flavor.

Preheat Grill or Pan:
- Preheat your grill or grill pan over medium-high heat.

Thread Chicken onto Skewers:
- Thread the marinated chicken pieces onto the skewers.

Cook Chicken Skewers:
- Brush the grill grates with oil to prevent sticking. Grill the chicken skewers for about 5-7 minutes per side or until fully cooked, basting with the reserved teriyaki marinade during grilling.

Check for Doneness:
- Ensure that the chicken reaches an internal temperature of 165°F (74°C) and is no longer pink in the center.

Garnish (Optional):
- Sprinkle sesame seeds and chopped green onions over the cooked chicken skewers for garnish.

Serve:
- Arrange the teriyaki chicken skewers on a platter and serve them hot. You can also serve with extra teriyaki sauce on the side for dipping.

These teriyaki chicken skewers are a savory and flavorful dish that works well as an appetizer or a main course. Enjoy the delicious combination of sweet and savory teriyaki sauce with tender grilled chicken!

Grilled Vegetable Antipasto Platter

Ingredients:

For Grilled Vegetables:

- Zucchini, sliced lengthwise
- Eggplant, sliced into rounds
- Bell peppers, halved and seeds removed
- Cherry tomatoes
- Red onion, sliced into rings
- Asparagus spears, trimmed
- Olive oil for brushing
- Salt and pepper to taste
- Balsamic glaze for drizzling (optional)

For Antipasto Platter:

- Marinated artichoke hearts
- Kalamata olives
- Green olives
- Sun-dried tomatoes
- Prosciutto or other cured meats
- Fresh mozzarella or feta cheese, cubed
- Bocconcini (small mozzarella balls)
- Italian bread or baguette slices, toasted

For Herb-infused Olive Oil:

- Extra virgin olive oil
- Fresh herbs such as rosemary, thyme, and oregano
- Garlic cloves, crushed
- Red pepper flakes (optional)
- Salt and pepper to taste

Instructions:

Preheat Grill:
- Preheat your grill to medium-high heat.

Grill Vegetables:
- Brush the sliced zucchini, eggplant, bell peppers, cherry tomatoes, red onion, and asparagus with olive oil. Season with salt and pepper.
- Grill the vegetables until they have grill marks and are tender. The cooking time will vary for each vegetable; generally, it takes about 4-5 minutes for zucchini and eggplant, 8-10 minutes for bell peppers, and 3-4 minutes for cherry tomatoes and asparagus.
- Remove the grilled vegetables from the heat and let them cool slightly.

Prepare Herb-infused Olive Oil:
- In a small bowl, combine extra virgin olive oil with fresh herbs, crushed garlic, red pepper flakes (if using), salt, and pepper. Allow the flavors to infuse.

Assemble Antipasto Platter:
- Arrange the grilled vegetables on a serving platter along with marinated artichoke hearts, Kalamata olives, green olives, sun-dried tomatoes, prosciutto, fresh mozzarella or feta cheese, bocconcini, and toasted bread slices.

Drizzle with Olive Oil:
- Drizzle the herb-infused olive oil over the grilled vegetables and other components of the platter. Optionally, you can also drizzle balsamic glaze over the grilled vegetables.

Serve:
- Serve the grilled vegetable antipasto platter as a vibrant and flavorful appetizer.

This grilled vegetable antipasto platter is not only visually appealing but also a wonderful medley of smoky grilled flavors and various textures. It's perfect for sharing and makes a great addition to any gathering or party. Enjoy!

Cherry Tomato and Mozzarella Bites

Ingredients:

- Cherry tomatoes
- Fresh mozzarella balls (bocconcini)
- Fresh basil leaves
- Balsamic glaze
- Extra virgin olive oil
- Salt and pepper to taste
- Toothpicks or small skewers

Instructions:

Prepare Tomatoes and Mozzarella:
- Wash the cherry tomatoes and cut them in half.
- Drain the fresh mozzarella balls if they are in liquid.

Assemble Bites:
- Take a toothpick or small skewer and thread a half cherry tomato, followed by a fresh basil leaf, and then a mozzarella ball. Repeat until you have as many bites as desired.

Arrange on a Platter:
- Arrange the assembled cherry tomato and mozzarella bites on a serving platter.

Drizzle with Olive Oil and Balsamic Glaze:
- Drizzle extra virgin olive oil and balsamic glaze over the bites. The combination of these two adds a wonderful flavor to the dish.

Season with Salt and Pepper:
- Sprinkle a pinch of salt and pepper over the bites to enhance the flavors.

Garnish (Optional):
- Garnish with additional fresh basil leaves for a decorative touch.

Serve:
- Serve the cherry tomato and mozzarella bites immediately. They can be enjoyed at room temperature or slightly chilled.

These cherry tomato and mozzarella bites are not only visually appealing but also bursting with the flavors of ripe tomatoes, creamy mozzarella, and fragrant basil. They make a perfect appetizer for parties, picnics, or any occasion where you want a light and refreshing bite. Enjoy!

Spinach and Artichoke Stuffed Mini Peppers

Ingredients:

- Mini sweet peppers (assorted colors)
- 1 cup fresh spinach, finely chopped
- 1/2 cup artichoke hearts, finely chopped (canned or jarred, drained)
- 1/2 cup cream cheese, softened
- 1/2 cup grated Parmesan cheese
- 1/4 cup mayonnaise
- 1 clove garlic, minced
- 1/4 teaspoon onion powder
- Salt and pepper to taste
- Olive oil for brushing
- Fresh parsley for garnish (optional)

Instructions:

Preheat Oven:
- Preheat your oven to 375°F (190°C).

Prepare Peppers:
- Cut the mini peppers in half lengthwise and remove the seeds and membranes.

Make the Filling:
- In a mixing bowl, combine chopped spinach, chopped artichoke hearts, cream cheese, grated Parmesan, mayonnaise, minced garlic, onion powder, salt, and pepper. Mix until well combined.

Stuff the Peppers:
- Spoon the spinach and artichoke filling into each pepper half, pressing down slightly.

Arrange on a Baking Sheet:
- Place the stuffed mini peppers on a baking sheet lined with parchment paper or lightly greased.

Brush with Olive Oil:
- Lightly brush the tops of the stuffed peppers with olive oil. This helps them to brown nicely in the oven.

Bake:
- Bake in the preheated oven for about 15-20 minutes or until the peppers are tender and the filling is golden brown on top.

Garnish (Optional):
- Garnish the stuffed peppers with fresh parsley for a pop of color.

Serve:
- Arrange the spinach and artichoke stuffed mini peppers on a serving platter and serve warm.

These stuffed mini peppers are a delightful combination of sweet, savory, and creamy flavors. They make a great finger food for parties or a delicious appetizer for any occasion. Enjoy!

Seared Scallops with Lemon Butter

Ingredients:

- Fresh scallops (about 1 pound)
- Salt and pepper to taste
- 2 tablespoons olive oil or clarified butter (ghee)
- 2 cloves garlic, minced
- Zest of 1 lemon
- Juice of 1 lemon
- 3 tablespoons unsalted butter
- Fresh parsley, chopped for garnish

Instructions:

Prepare Scallops:
- Pat the scallops dry with paper towels to remove excess moisture. Season both sides with salt and pepper.

Heat Pan:
- Heat a large skillet or non-stick pan over medium-high heat.

Sear Scallops:
- Add olive oil or clarified butter to the hot pan. Place the scallops in the pan, making sure not to overcrowd them. Allow them to sear without moving for about 2-3 minutes or until a golden crust forms.

Flip Scallops:
- Carefully flip the scallops using tongs and sear on the other side for an additional 2-3 minutes or until cooked through. The centers should be opaque and the edges should be golden brown.

Remove Scallops:
- Transfer the seared scallops to a plate and cover with foil to keep them warm.

Make Lemon Butter Sauce:
- In the same pan, add minced garlic and cook for about 30 seconds until fragrant. Be careful not to burn the garlic.
- Add lemon zest and lemon juice to the pan. Stir to deglaze the pan and incorporate the flavors.

Finish the Sauce:

- Reduce the heat to low, and add unsalted butter to the pan. Swirl the pan to melt the butter and create a creamy lemon butter sauce. Season the sauce with salt and pepper to taste.

Serve:
- Pour the lemon butter sauce over the seared scallops. Garnish with fresh chopped parsley.

Enjoy:
- Serve the seared scallops with lemon butter immediately. They are delicious on their own or can be paired with a side of risotto, pasta, or a fresh salad.

This dish is perfect for a special dinner or when you want to impress with a quick and tasty seafood recipe. The combination of seared scallops and zesty lemon butter is simply irresistible. Enjoy!

Apricot and Brie Puff Pastry Bites

Ingredients:

- 1 sheet of puff pastry, thawed if frozen
- Apricot preserves or jam
- Brie cheese, cut into small cubes
- Fresh thyme leaves for garnish (optional)
- Honey for drizzling (optional)

Instructions:

Preheat Oven:
- Preheat your oven to the temperature specified on the puff pastry package (usually around 375°F or 190°C).

Roll Out Puff Pastry:
- Roll out the puff pastry sheet on a lightly floured surface to smooth out any creases.

Cut Into Squares:
- Using a sharp knife or a pizza cutter, cut the puff pastry into squares, approximately 2 inches by 2 inches.

Assemble the Bites:
- Place a small cube of Brie in the center of each puff pastry square.
- Spoon a small amount of apricot preserves or jam on top of the Brie.

Fold and Seal:
- Fold the corners of each puff pastry square towards the center, creating a little pocket. Press the edges to seal.

Place on Baking Sheet:
- Arrange the filled puff pastry bites on a baking sheet lined with parchment paper.

Bake:
- Bake in the preheated oven for about 12-15 minutes or until the puff pastry is golden brown and puffed up.

Garnish:
- If desired, garnish each puff pastry bite with fresh thyme leaves and drizzle with honey for an extra touch of sweetness.

Serve:
- Allow the apricot and Brie puff pastry bites to cool slightly before serving.

These bites are a delightful appetizer for parties, brunches, or any special occasion. The combination of the creamy Brie, sweet apricot, and flaky puff pastry creates a delicious treat that's sure to be a crowd-pleaser. Enjoy!

Garlic and Herb Marinated Feta Cubes

Ingredients:

- 8 ounces feta cheese, cut into cubes
- 2 cloves garlic, minced
- 1 teaspoon dried oregano
- 1 teaspoon dried thyme
- 1 teaspoon dried rosemary
- 1/2 teaspoon red pepper flakes (optional for a bit of heat)
- Zest of 1 lemon
- Freshly ground black pepper to taste
- Extra virgin olive oil

Instructions:

Prepare Feta Cubes:
- Cut the feta cheese into bite-sized cubes.

Make Marinade:
- In a bowl, combine minced garlic, dried oregano, dried thyme, dried rosemary, red pepper flakes (if using), lemon zest, and freshly ground black pepper.

Marinate Feta:
- Place the feta cubes in a shallow dish or a jar. Pour the marinade over the feta, ensuring each cube is well-coated. Gently toss the feta to distribute the herbs evenly.

Cover and Refrigerate:
- Cover the dish or jar and refrigerate for at least 2 hours or overnight. This allows the feta to absorb the flavors of the marinade.

Bring to Room Temperature:
- Before serving, let the marinated feta come to room temperature for the best flavor.

Drizzle with Olive Oil:
- Just before serving, drizzle extra virgin olive oil over the marinated feta cubes. The olive oil adds richness and helps preserve the feta.

Serve:

- Arrange the garlic and herb marinated feta cubes on a serving platter. You can use toothpicks for easy serving or serve them in a bowl with crusty bread on the side.

These marinated feta cubes are a fantastic addition to a cheese board, antipasto platter, or as a standalone appetizer. The combination of garlic, herbs, and the tangy creaminess of feta creates a delightful burst of flavors. Enjoy!

Chicken Satay with Peanut Dipping Sauce

Ingredients:

For Chicken Satay:

- 1.5 pounds boneless, skinless chicken breasts or thighs, cut into thin strips
- 1/4 cup soy sauce
- 2 tablespoons fish sauce
- 2 tablespoons brown sugar
- 1 tablespoon curry powder
- 1 teaspoon turmeric
- 2 cloves garlic, minced
- 1 tablespoon vegetable oil
- Wooden skewers, soaked in water for 30 minutes

For Peanut Dipping Sauce:

- 1/2 cup peanut butter
- 3 tablespoons soy sauce
- 2 tablespoons rice vinegar
- 2 tablespoons brown sugar
- 1 tablespoon sesame oil
- 1 teaspoon grated fresh ginger
- 1 clove garlic, minced
- Water (as needed to adjust consistency)

Instructions:

For Chicken Satay:

    Prepare Marinade:
- In a bowl, whisk together soy sauce, fish sauce, brown sugar, curry powder, turmeric, minced garlic, and vegetable oil to make the marinade.

    Marinate Chicken:

- Place the chicken strips in a shallow dish and pour half of the marinade over them. Toss to coat the chicken evenly. Reserve the remaining marinade for basting.

Thread Chicken onto Skewers:
- Thread the marinated chicken strips onto the soaked wooden skewers.

Grill or Pan-Sear:
- Grill the chicken skewers on a preheated grill or pan over medium-high heat. Cook for about 3-4 minutes per side or until the chicken is cooked through and has a nice char.

Baste with Marinade:
- While grilling, baste the chicken with the reserved marinade to add more flavor.

For Peanut Dipping Sauce:

Prepare Sauce:
- In a small saucepan over low heat, combine peanut butter, soy sauce, rice vinegar, brown sugar, sesame oil, grated ginger, and minced garlic. Stir continuously until the mixture is well combined and heated through.

Adjust Consistency:
- If the sauce is too thick, you can thin it with a little water until you reach your desired consistency.

Serve:
- Serve the chicken satay skewers hot with the peanut dipping sauce on the side.

These chicken satay skewers with peanut dipping sauce are perfect for parties, barbecues, or as a flavorful appetizer. The combination of the savory, sweet, and slightly spicy chicken with the creamy peanut sauce is simply irresistible. Enjoy!

Pomegranate and Goat Cheese Crostini

Ingredients:

- Baguette or French bread, thinly sliced
- Goat cheese (chevre)
- Pomegranate seeds
- Honey, for drizzling
- Fresh thyme leaves for garnish (optional)

Instructions:

Preheat Oven:
- Preheat your oven to 375°F (190°C).

Slice and Toast Baguette:
- Slice the baguette into thin rounds. Place the slices on a baking sheet and toast them in the preheated oven until they are golden brown and crisp, usually for about 5-7 minutes. Keep an eye on them to prevent burning.

Spread Goat Cheese:
- Once the baguette slices are toasted, spread a layer of goat cheese on each slice while they are still warm.

Add Pomegranate Seeds:
- Sprinkle a generous amount of fresh pomegranate seeds on top of the goat cheese.

Drizzle with Honey:
- Drizzle honey over the crostini for a touch of sweetness. The honey complements the tanginess of the goat cheese and the burst of juiciness from the pomegranate seeds.

Garnish (Optional):
- Garnish each crostini with fresh thyme leaves for a pop of color and additional flavor.

Serve:
- Arrange the pomegranate and goat cheese crostini on a serving platter and serve immediately.

These crostini make for a visually stunning and delicious appetizer that's perfect for holiday gatherings, parties, or any special occasion. The combination of creamy goat cheese, juicy pomegranate seeds, and the sweetness of honey creates a delightful flavor profile. Enjoy!

Olive Tapenade on Crostini

Ingredients:

For Olive Tapenade:

- 1 cup pitted Kalamata olives
- 1/2 cup green olives (pitted)
- 2 tablespoons capers, drained
- 2 cloves garlic, minced
- 2 teaspoons Dijon mustard
- 2 tablespoons fresh parsley, chopped
- 1 tablespoon fresh lemon juice
- 1/4 cup extra virgin olive oil
- Freshly ground black pepper, to taste

For Crostini:

- Baguette or French bread, thinly sliced
- Olive oil for brushing

Instructions:

For Olive Tapenade:

Prepare Olives:
- Rinse and drain the Kalamata and green olives.

Blend Ingredients:
- In a food processor, combine Kalamata olives, green olives, capers, minced garlic, Dijon mustard, fresh parsley, and fresh lemon juice. Pulse until the mixture is coarsely chopped.

Add Olive Oil:
- With the food processor running, slowly drizzle in the extra virgin olive oil until the tapenade reaches your desired consistency. It should be a bit chunky, not completely smooth.

Season with Pepper:

- Season the tapenade with freshly ground black pepper to taste. Remember that olives and capers are already salty, so additional salt may not be necessary.

For Crostini:

Preheat Oven:
- Preheat your oven to 375°F (190°C).

Slice and Toast Baguette:
- Slice the baguette into thin rounds. Place the slices on a baking sheet and brush one side with olive oil. Toast in the preheated oven until golden brown, about 5-7 minutes. Keep an eye on them to avoid burning.

Serve:
- Once the crostini are done, let them cool slightly. Spread a generous amount of olive tapenade on each crostini.

Garnish (Optional):
- Garnish with additional chopped parsley or a drizzle of extra virgin olive oil.

Serve:
- Arrange the olive tapenade crostini on a serving platter and serve at room temperature.

This olive tapenade on crostini is a savory and briny appetizer that's perfect for entertaining or enjoying a simple snack. The combination of olives, capers, and fresh herbs creates a burst of Mediterranean flavors. Enjoy!

Gourmet Deviled Quail Eggs

Ingredients:

For Deviled Quail Eggs:

- 12 quail eggs
- 2 tablespoons mayonnaise
- 1 teaspoon Dijon mustard
- 1 teaspoon white wine vinegar
- 1 tablespoon fresh chives, finely chopped
- Salt and pepper to taste
- Paprika or cayenne pepper for garnish (optional)

For Garnish (Optional):

- Fresh chives, chopped
- Microgreens or herbs for decoration

Instructions:

Boil Quail Eggs:
- Bring a pot of water to a boil. Gently place the quail eggs into the boiling water using a slotted spoon. Boil for about 2 minutes for soft-boiled eggs or 4 minutes for hard-boiled eggs.

Cool and Peel:
- Transfer the boiled quail eggs to a bowl of ice water to cool quickly. Once cooled, carefully peel the eggs. Quail eggs have delicate shells, so be gentle during the peeling process.

Slice Eggs:
- Slice each quail egg in half lengthwise, revealing the yolk and whites.

Remove Yolks:
- Carefully remove the yolks from the quail egg halves and place them in a separate bowl.

Make Deviled Egg Filling:

- Mash the quail egg yolks with a fork. Add mayonnaise, Dijon mustard, white wine vinegar, and finely chopped chives. Mix until you have a smooth and creamy filling. Season with salt and pepper to taste.

Fill Egg Whites:
- Using a small spoon or piping bag, fill each quail egg white half with the deviled egg filling.

Garnish:
- Garnish the deviled quail eggs with a sprinkle of paprika or cayenne pepper for a touch of heat. Optionally, add chopped fresh chives or microgreens for decoration.

Serve:
- Arrange the deviled quail eggs on a serving platter and serve them chilled.

These gourmet deviled quail eggs make for an elegant and bite-sized appetizer that's perfect for special occasions or upscale gatherings. The miniature size and rich flavor of quail eggs add a unique twist to the classic deviled egg. Enjoy!

Rosemary and Sea Salt Marcona Almonds

Ingredients:

- 1 cup Marcona almonds
- 1 tablespoon fresh rosemary, finely chopped
- 1 tablespoon extra virgin olive oil
- Sea salt, to taste

Instructions:

Preheat Oven:
- Preheat your oven to 350°F (175°C).

Prepare Rosemary:
- Finely chop fresh rosemary until you have about 1 tablespoon.

Toss Almonds with Olive Oil:
- In a bowl, toss the Marcona almonds with extra virgin olive oil until they are evenly coated.

Add Rosemary:
- Sprinkle the finely chopped rosemary over the almonds and toss again to distribute the rosemary evenly.

Spread on Baking Sheet:
- Spread the rosemary-coated Marcona almonds in a single layer on a baking sheet lined with parchment paper.

Bake:
- Bake in the preheated oven for about 10-12 minutes, or until the almonds are golden and fragrant. Keep an eye on them to prevent burning.

Season with Sea Salt:
- While the almonds are still warm from the oven, sprinkle them with sea salt to taste. Toss gently to coat the almonds in the salt.

Cool:
- Allow the rosemary and sea salt Marcona almonds to cool completely before serving. They will continue to crisp up as they cool.

Serve:
- Once cooled, transfer the almonds to a serving bowl. They are ready to be enjoyed as a delicious and fragrant snack.

These rosemary and sea salt Marcona almonds are a delightful combination of savory and aromatic flavors. They make an excellent appetizer or party snack and are sure to impress with their gourmet touch. Enjoy!

Gruyere and Caramelized Onion Puffs

Ingredients:

For Caramelized Onions:

- 2 large onions, thinly sliced
- 2 tablespoons unsalted butter
- 1 tablespoon olive oil
- Salt and pepper to taste
- 1 teaspoon balsamic vinegar (optional, for extra flavor)

For Gruyere and Caramelized Onion Puffs:

- 1 sheet puff pastry, thawed if frozen
- 1 cup Gruyere cheese, grated
- Caramelized onions (from the previous step)
- Fresh thyme leaves for garnish (optional)
- Egg wash (1 egg beaten with 1 tablespoon water)

Instructions:

For Caramelized Onions:

Caramelize Onions:
- In a large skillet, heat butter and olive oil over medium-low heat. Add the thinly sliced onions and cook, stirring occasionally, until the onions are golden brown and caramelized. This process can take about 20-30 minutes.
- Season with salt and pepper to taste. Optionally, add balsamic vinegar for extra depth of flavor. Set aside to cool.

For Gruyere and Caramelized Onion Puffs:

Preheat Oven:
- Preheat your oven to 400°F (200°C).

Roll Out Puff Pastry:

- Roll out the puff pastry sheet on a lightly floured surface to smooth out any creases.

Cut Into Squares:
- Cut the puff pastry into squares, approximately 2 inches by 2 inches.

Assemble Puffs:
- Place a small amount of caramelized onions in the center of each puff pastry square. Top with a generous pinch of grated Gruyere cheese.

Fold and Seal:
- Fold the corners of each puff pastry square towards the center, creating a little pocket. Press the edges to seal.

Brush with Egg Wash:
- Brush the tops of the puff pastry puffs with the egg wash. This will give them a beautiful golden color when baked.

Bake:
- Place the assembled Gruyere and caramelized onion puffs on a baking sheet lined with parchment paper. Bake in the preheated oven for about 15-20 minutes or until the puffs are golden brown and puffed up.

Garnish (Optional):
- Garnish with fresh thyme leaves for a pop of color and added flavor.

Serve:
- Allow the Gruyere and caramelized onion puffs to cool for a few minutes before serving. They can be served warm or at room temperature.

These Gruyere and caramelized onion puffs are a savory and elegant appetizer that's perfect for parties, gatherings, or as a tasty snack. The combination of sweet caramelized onions and rich Gruyere cheese in a flaky puff pastry creates a mouthwatering treat. Enjoy!

Tuna Tartare with Avocado

Ingredients:

- 1/2 pound sushi-grade tuna, finely diced
- 1 ripe avocado, diced
- 2 tablespoons soy sauce
- 1 tablespoon sesame oil
- 1 tablespoon fresh lime juice
- 1 teaspoon fresh ginger, minced
- 1 teaspoon honey or agave nectar
- 1 green onion, finely chopped
- Sesame seeds for garnish
- Nori strips (seaweed), for serving (optional)
- Wonton crisps or crackers, for serving

Instructions:

Prepare Tuna and Avocado:
- Ensure that the tuna is very fresh and sushi-grade. Dice the tuna into small, uniform cubes. Dice the ripe avocado into similar-sized cubes.

Make Tartare Mixture:
- In a bowl, gently combine the diced tuna and avocado.

Prepare Dressing:
- In a separate small bowl, whisk together soy sauce, sesame oil, fresh lime juice, minced ginger, and honey or agave nectar to create the dressing.

Combine and Season:
- Pour the dressing over the tuna and avocado mixture. Add finely chopped green onion. Gently toss the ingredients until evenly coated. Be careful not to mash the avocado.

Chill:
- Cover the bowl with plastic wrap and let the tuna tartare mixture chill in the refrigerator for at least 15-30 minutes. This allows the flavors to meld.

Serve:
- Spoon the chilled tuna tartare into serving dishes. Optionally, you can use a ring mold for a neat presentation.

Garnish:

- Garnish the tuna tartare with sesame seeds. You can also add nori strips for an extra touch of flavor and presentation.

Serve with Wonton Crisps:
- Accompany the tuna tartare with wonton crisps or your choice of crackers for scooping.

Enjoy:
- Serve the tuna tartare with avocado immediately and enjoy the freshness of the dish.

This tuna tartare with avocado is a light and flavorful appetizer that's perfect for special occasions or a light lunch. The combination of fresh tuna, creamy avocado, and the zesty dressing creates a harmonious and delicious dish.

Herbed Goat Cheese-Stuffed Cherry Tomatoes

Ingredients:

- Cherry tomatoes
- Goat cheese (chevre), softened
- Fresh herbs (e.g., basil, chives, thyme), finely chopped
- Salt and black pepper to taste
- Extra virgin olive oil for drizzling (optional)
- Balsamic glaze for drizzling (optional)

Instructions:

Prepare Cherry Tomatoes:
- Wash and dry the cherry tomatoes. Cut a small slice off the top of each tomato to create a flat base, allowing them to stand upright.

Make Herbed Goat Cheese Filling:
- In a bowl, combine softened goat cheese with finely chopped fresh herbs of your choice. Common choices include basil, chives, and thyme. Mix until the herbs are evenly distributed throughout the goat cheese.

Season:
- Season the herbed goat cheese mixture with salt and black pepper to taste. Adjust the seasoning according to your preference.

Stuff the Tomatoes:
- Using a small spoon or a piping bag, fill each cherry tomato with the herbed goat cheese mixture. You can choose to make a simple mound on top or get creative with piping.

Drizzle with Olive Oil and Balsamic Glaze (Optional):
- For added flavor, you can drizzle the stuffed cherry tomatoes with extra virgin olive oil and balsamic glaze. This step is optional but enhances the overall taste and presentation.

Chill (Optional):
- If time allows, refrigerate the stuffed cherry tomatoes for about 30 minutes to allow the flavors to meld and the cheese to firm up slightly.

Serve:
- Arrange the herbed goat cheese-stuffed cherry tomatoes on a serving platter and serve immediately.

These herbed goat cheese-stuffed cherry tomatoes are a delightful, bite-sized appetizer that combines the sweetness of cherry tomatoes with the creamy and herby goodness of goat cheese. They make a colorful and elegant addition to any gathering or party. Enjoy!

Lobster Salad in Endive Spears

Ingredients:

For Lobster Salad:

- 1 1/2 cups cooked lobster meat, diced
- 1/4 cup mayonnaise
- 1 tablespoon fresh lemon juice
- 1 celery stalk, finely chopped
- 2 tablespoons fresh chives, chopped
- Salt and black pepper to taste

For Endive Spears:

- Endive heads, separated into individual leaves

Instructions:

For Lobster Salad:

Prepare Lobster:
- If you haven't already, cook the lobster and dice the meat. You can use pre-cooked lobster or cook it yourself.

Make Lobster Salad:
- In a bowl, combine the diced lobster meat with mayonnaise, fresh lemon juice, finely chopped celery, and chopped chives. Mix well to coat the lobster evenly.

Season:
- Season the lobster salad with salt and black pepper to taste. Adjust the seasoning according to your preference.

Chill:
- Cover the bowl and let the lobster salad chill in the refrigerator for at least 30 minutes to allow the flavors to meld.

For Endive Spears:

Separate Endive Leaves:
- Carefully separate the leaves of the endive heads, creating individual "boats" for serving.

Assembly:

Fill Endive Spears:
- Spoon a portion of the chilled lobster salad into each endive spear, filling them generously.

Garnish (Optional):
- Garnish the lobster salad in endive spears with additional chopped chives for a pop of color and flavor.

Serve:
- Arrange the filled endive spears on a serving platter and serve immediately.

This lobster salad in endive spears is an elegant and light appetizer, perfect for special occasions or gatherings. The sweet and succulent lobster pairs beautifully with the crisp and slightly bitter endive, creating a harmonious blend of flavors and textures. Enjoy!

Honey Sriracha Glazed Meatballs

Ingredients:

For the Meatballs:

- 1 pound ground meat (beef, pork, chicken, or a combination)
- 1/2 cup breadcrumbs
- 1/4 cup finely chopped onion
- 2 cloves garlic, minced
- 1 large egg
- 1 tablespoon soy sauce
- Salt and pepper to taste
- 1 tablespoon vegetable oil (for cooking)

For the Honey Sriracha Glaze:

- 1/4 cup honey
- 2 tablespoons Sriracha sauce (adjust to taste)
- 2 tablespoons soy sauce
- 1 tablespoon rice vinegar
- 1 teaspoon sesame oil (optional, for extra flavor)
- Sesame seeds and chopped green onions for garnish (optional)

Instructions:

For the Meatballs:

Preheat Oven:
- Preheat your oven to 400°F (200°C).

Mix Meatball Ingredients:
- In a large bowl, combine ground meat, breadcrumbs, chopped onion, minced garlic, egg, soy sauce, salt, and pepper. Mix until well combined.

Shape Meatballs:
- Form the mixture into bite-sized meatballs, about 1 inch in diameter.

Cook Meatballs:

- Heat vegetable oil in an oven-safe skillet over medium-high heat. Brown the meatballs on all sides, turning as needed.

Transfer to Oven:
- Once browned, transfer the skillet to the preheated oven and bake for about 12-15 minutes or until the meatballs are cooked through.

For the Honey Sriracha Glaze:

Prepare Glaze:
- While the meatballs are baking, prepare the glaze. In a small saucepan, combine honey, Sriracha sauce, soy sauce, rice vinegar, and sesame oil. Heat over medium heat, stirring until the ingredients are well combined and the mixture slightly thickens.

Glaze Meatballs:
- Once the meatballs are cooked, remove them from the oven. Pour the Honey Sriracha glaze over the meatballs, ensuring they are well coated.

Garnish (Optional):
- Garnish with sesame seeds and chopped green onions for added flavor and presentation.

Serve:
- Serve the Honey Sriracha glazed meatballs immediately. They can be served with toothpicks for easy snacking.

These Honey Sriracha glazed meatballs are a crowd-pleaser, combining the sweetness of honey with the kick of Sriracha. They make a fantastic appetizer for parties or a tasty addition to your game day spread. Enjoy!

Roasted Red Pepper Hummus Cups

Ingredients:

- 1 cup roasted red pepper hummus (store-bought or homemade)
- Mini phyllo cups (available in the frozen section of most grocery stores)
- Fresh parsley or cilantro for garnish (optional)
- Olive oil for drizzling (optional)
- Paprika for sprinkling (optional)

Instructions:

Thaw Phyllo Cups:
- If using frozen mini phyllo cups, follow the package instructions to thaw them. Typically, they need to be baked in the oven for a few minutes.

Fill Cups with Hummus:
- Spoon or pipe the roasted red pepper hummus into each mini phyllo cup. Fill them just enough to create a small mound on top.

Garnish (Optional):
- If desired, garnish each hummus cup with fresh parsley or cilantro for a pop of color.

Drizzle with Olive Oil (Optional):
- For added richness, drizzle a little bit of olive oil over the top of the hummus cups. This step is optional but enhances the flavor.

Sprinkle with Paprika (Optional):
- If you like a bit of spice and additional color, sprinkle a pinch of paprika over the hummus cups.

Serve:
- Arrange the roasted red pepper hummus cups on a serving platter and serve immediately.

These roasted red pepper hummus cups are not only visually appealing but also delicious and convenient. They make a great finger food for parties, gatherings, or as an appetizer before a meal. The combination of the smoky roasted red pepper flavor and the creamy hummus is sure to be a hit. Enjoy!

Coconut Shrimp with Mango Salsa

Ingredients:

For Coconut Shrimp:

- 1 pound large shrimp, peeled and deveined
- 1 cup sweetened shredded coconut
- 1 cup panko breadcrumbs
- 1/2 cup all-purpose flour
- 2 large eggs
- Salt and pepper to taste
- Vegetable oil for frying

For Mango Salsa:

- 1 ripe mango, diced
- 1/2 red bell pepper, diced
- 1/4 cup red onion, finely chopped
- 1/4 cup fresh cilantro, chopped
- Juice of 1 lime
- Salt and pepper to taste

Instructions:

For Coconut Shrimp:

    Prepare Shrimp:
- Pat the shrimp dry with paper towels. Season with salt and pepper.

    Set Up Breading Station:
- In three separate shallow bowls, place flour in one, beaten eggs in another, and a mixture of shredded coconut and panko breadcrumbs in the third.

    Coat Shrimp:
- Dip each shrimp into the flour, shaking off excess. Then, dip into the beaten eggs, and finally, coat with the coconut and breadcrumb mixture, pressing gently to adhere.

    Fry Shrimp:
- In a large skillet, heat vegetable oil over medium-high heat. Fry the coated shrimp for about 2-3 minutes on each side or until golden brown and

crispy. Work in batches to avoid overcrowding the pan. Transfer the cooked shrimp to a paper towel-lined plate to absorb excess oil.

For Mango Salsa:

Prepare Mango Salsa:
- In a bowl, combine diced mango, red bell pepper, red onion, cilantro, lime juice, salt, and pepper. Mix well to combine.

Chill Salsa:
- Allow the mango salsa to chill in the refrigerator for at least 15-30 minutes to let the flavors meld.

Assemble and Serve:

Arrange:
- Arrange the coconut shrimp on a serving platter.

Serve with Mango Salsa:
- Serve the coconut shrimp with a side of chilled mango salsa.

Garnish (Optional):
- Optionally, garnish with additional cilantro or lime wedges for a fresh touch.

These coconut shrimp with mango salsa are a perfect combination of crunchy, sweet, and tangy flavors. They make a fantastic appetizer for summer parties or any tropical-themed gathering. Enjoy!

Pistachio and Cranberry Goat Cheese Balls

Ingredients:

- 8 ounces goat cheese, softened
- 1/2 cup dried cranberries, finely chopped
- 1/2 cup pistachios, finely chopped
- 1 tablespoon honey
- 1/4 teaspoon black pepper (optional, for a hint of heat)
- Crackers or sliced baguette for serving

Instructions:

Prepare Goat Cheese Mixture:
- In a bowl, combine softened goat cheese, finely chopped dried cranberries, finely chopped pistachios, honey, and black pepper (if using). Mix well until all ingredients are evenly incorporated.

Chill Mixture:
- Place the goat cheese mixture in the refrigerator for about 15-30 minutes. This will make it easier to handle and shape into balls.

Shape into Balls:
- After chilling, scoop out portions of the mixture and roll them into small bite-sized balls using your hands. Aim for uniform size for a consistent presentation.

Coat with Pistachios:
- Roll each goat cheese ball in additional finely chopped pistachios to coat them thoroughly. Press the pistachios onto the balls to ensure they adhere well.

Chill Again (Optional):
- If time allows, you can chill the pistachio and cranberry goat cheese balls for another 15-30 minutes to firm them up slightly before serving.

Serve:
- Arrange the pistachio and cranberry goat cheese balls on a serving platter.

Serve with Crackers or Baguette:
- Serve the goat cheese balls with your choice of crackers or sliced baguette.

These pistachio and cranberry goat cheese balls make a delightful and visually appealing appetizer for holiday gatherings, parties, or any special occasion. The combination of creamy goat cheese, sweet cranberries, and crunchy pistachios creates a burst of flavors and textures. Enjoy!

White Truffle and Parmesan Popcorn

Ingredients:

- 1/2 cup popcorn kernels (or 12 cups popped popcorn)
- 2 tablespoons white truffle oil
- 1/2 cup grated Parmesan cheese
- 2 tablespoons unsalted butter, melted
- Salt, to taste
- Fresh parsley, chopped (optional, for garnish)

Instructions:

Pop the Popcorn:
- If using popcorn kernels, pop them using your preferred method—air popper, stovetop, or microwave. Ensure they are fully popped and set aside.

Prepare Truffle and Parmesan Mixture:
- In a small bowl, mix the white truffle oil and melted butter together.

Coat the Popcorn:
- Drizzle the truffle and butter mixture over the popped popcorn. Toss the popcorn gently to ensure an even coating.

Add Parmesan Cheese:
- Sprinkle the grated Parmesan cheese over the popcorn. Toss again to distribute the cheese evenly.

Season with Salt:
- Season the truffle and Parmesan popcorn with salt to taste. Keep in mind that Parmesan adds saltiness, so adjust accordingly.

Garnish (Optional):
- If desired, garnish the popcorn with chopped fresh parsley for a burst of color and added freshness.

Serve:
- Transfer the white truffle and Parmesan popcorn to a large bowl or individual serving bowls.

Enjoy:
- Enjoy this gourmet popcorn as a luxurious snack for movie nights, parties, or any occasion.

The combination of white truffle oil, Parmesan cheese, and butter elevates this popcorn to a whole new level of sophistication. It's a perfect blend of savory, nutty, and cheesy flavors. This gourmet popcorn is sure to be a hit with anyone who enjoys a touch of luxury in their snacks.

Sherry-infused Mushroom Crostini

Ingredients:

For the Mushroom Topping:

- 2 cups mushrooms (cremini, shiitake, or a mix), finely chopped
- 2 tablespoons olive oil
- 2 cloves garlic, minced
- 1/4 cup dry sherry
- Salt and black pepper to taste
- Fresh thyme leaves for garnish (optional)

For the Crostini:

- Baguette or French bread, thinly sliced
- Olive oil for brushing
- 1 clove garlic, peeled (for rubbing on the crostini)

Instructions:

For the Mushroom Topping:

Sauté Mushrooms:
- In a skillet, heat olive oil over medium heat. Add the minced garlic and sauté for a minute until fragrant.

Add Mushrooms:
- Add the finely chopped mushrooms to the skillet. Cook until the mushrooms release their moisture and become golden brown.

Deglaze with Sherry:
- Pour in the dry sherry to deglaze the pan, scraping up any browned bits from the bottom. Allow the sherry to cook off, leaving behind a rich flavor.

Season:
- Season the mushrooms with salt and black pepper to taste. Cook for an additional 2-3 minutes until any remaining liquid evaporates.

Garnish (Optional):

- If desired, garnish the mushroom mixture with fresh thyme leaves for an extra layer of flavor.

For the Crostini:

Preheat Oven:
- Preheat your oven to 375°F (190°C).

Slice and Toast Baguette:
- Slice the baguette into thin rounds. Place the slices on a baking sheet and brush one side with olive oil. Toast in the preheated oven until golden brown, about 5-7 minutes. Remove from the oven.

Rub with Garlic:
- While the crostini are still warm, rub one side of each slice with the peeled clove of garlic. This imparts a subtle garlic flavor to the bread.

Assemble and Serve:

Top Crostini:
- Spoon a generous amount of the sherry-infused mushroom mixture onto each garlic-rubbed crostini.

Garnish (Optional):
- Garnish with additional fresh thyme leaves if desired.

Serve:
- Arrange the sherry-infused mushroom crostini on a serving platter and serve immediately.

These mushroom crostini with sherry are a sophisticated and flavorful appetizer, perfect for entertaining or special occasions. The combination of mushrooms, sherry, and garlic atop crispy bread creates a delightful bite that's sure to impress your guests. Enjoy!

Spicy Tuna Rolls in Cucumber Cups

Ingredients:

For the Spicy Tuna Filling:

- 1/2 pound sushi-grade tuna, finely diced
- 2 tablespoons mayonnaise
- 1 tablespoon Sriracha sauce (adjust to taste)
- 1 teaspoon soy sauce
- 1 teaspoon sesame oil
- 1 green onion, finely chopped
- Sesame seeds for garnish

For the Cucumber Cups:

- English cucumbers
- Salt

Optional Garnish:

- Avocado slices
- Radish slices
- Microgreens or sprouts
- Soy sauce and wasabi for serving

Instructions:

For the Spicy Tuna Filling:

> Prepare Tuna Mixture:
> - In a bowl, combine finely diced sushi-grade tuna, mayonnaise, Sriracha sauce, soy sauce, sesame oil, and chopped green onion. Mix until well combined.
>
> Chill Filling:
> - Cover the bowl with plastic wrap and let the spicy tuna filling chill in the refrigerator for at least 15-30 minutes. This allows the flavors to meld.

For the Cucumber Cups:

Slice Cucumbers:
- Cut the English cucumbers into thick slices, about 1 to 1.5 inches in thickness.

Hollow Out Centers:
- Using a melon baller or a teaspoon, hollow out the center of each cucumber slice to create a cup. Leave a base to hold the filling.

Sprinkle with Salt:
- Lightly sprinkle the inside of each cucumber cup with a bit of salt to enhance the flavor.

Assembly:

Fill Cucumber Cups:
- Spoon the chilled spicy tuna filling into each cucumber cup.

Garnish (Optional):
- Garnish with sesame seeds and add additional toppings like avocado slices, radish slices, or microgreens if desired.

Serve:
- Arrange the spicy tuna rolls in cucumber cups on a serving platter. Serve with soy sauce and wasabi on the side.

These spicy tuna rolls in cucumber cups make a light, refreshing, and visually appealing appetizer. They're perfect for a healthier option at parties or gatherings. The crispness of the cucumber complements the spicy tuna filling beautifully. Enjoy!

Watermelon Feta Mint Skewers

Ingredients:

- Watermelon, seedless, cut into bite-sized cubes
- Feta cheese, cut into small cubes
- Fresh mint leaves
- Balsamic glaze (optional, for drizzling)
- Toothpicks or small skewers

Instructions:

Prepare Ingredients:
- Cut the watermelon into bite-sized cubes. Cut the feta cheese into small cubes that are roughly the same size as the watermelon cubes.

Assemble Skewers:
- Take a toothpick or small skewer and thread on a cube of watermelon, followed by a cube of feta, and then a fresh mint leaf. Repeat until the skewer is filled.

Arrange on Serving Platter:
- Place the watermelon feta mint skewers on a serving platter. You can arrange them in a decorative pattern.

Drizzle with Balsamic Glaze (Optional):
- For an extra burst of flavor, drizzle balsamic glaze over the watermelon feta mint skewers just before serving. This step is optional but adds a delightful tangy sweetness.

Serve:
- Serve these skewers chilled for a refreshing and hydrating appetizer.

These watermelon feta mint skewers are a perfect combination of sweet, salty, and fresh flavors. They are great for summer gatherings, picnics, or as a light and healthy appetizer any time of the year. Enjoy the burst of colors and tastes in every bite!

Saffron and Lemon Risotto Balls

Ingredients:

For the Risotto:

- 1 cup Arborio rice
- 1/2 cup dry white wine
- 4 cups chicken or vegetable broth, kept warm
- 1 small onion, finely chopped
- 2 tablespoons unsalted butter
- 2 tablespoons olive oil
- 1/2 teaspoon saffron threads (soaked in 1 tablespoon warm water)
- Zest of 1 lemon
- 1/2 cup freshly grated Parmesan cheese
- Salt and black pepper to taste

For Coating and Frying:

- 2 cups breadcrumbs
- 3 large eggs, beaten
- Vegetable oil for frying

Instructions:

For the Risotto:

    Infuse Saffron:
- Soak saffron threads in 1 tablespoon of warm water and set aside.

    Prepare Risotto:
- In a large pan, heat the olive oil and 1 tablespoon of butter over medium heat. Add chopped onions and sauté until translucent.

    Add Rice and Toast:
- Add Arborio rice to the pan and cook, stirring constantly, until the rice is well-coated and slightly toasted.

    Deglaze with Wine:

- Pour in the white wine, stirring continuously until the wine is mostly absorbed by the rice.

Add Saffron and Lemon:
- Add the soaked saffron and its water, lemon zest, and a ladleful of warm broth to the rice. Stir and allow the liquid to be absorbed.

Continue Cooking:
- Continue adding the warm broth one ladleful at a time, stirring frequently and allowing the liquid to be absorbed before adding more. Cook the risotto until it's creamy and the rice is al dente.

Finish with Parmesan:
- Stir in the freshly grated Parmesan cheese, remaining butter, and season with salt and black pepper. Remove from heat and let the risotto cool.

Chill Risotto:
- Transfer the risotto to a shallow dish and let it cool completely. Refrigerate for at least 2 hours or until the mixture is firm enough to handle.

Assemble and Fry:

Shape Risotto Balls:
- Take a spoonful of the chilled risotto and shape it into a ball. Repeat until all the risotto is used.

Coat in Breadcrumbs:
- Dip each risotto ball into beaten eggs and then roll in breadcrumbs, ensuring they are evenly coated.

Heat Oil:
- In a deep pan, heat vegetable oil to 350°F (180°C).

Fry Risotto Balls:
- Carefully fry the risotto balls in batches until they are golden brown and crispy. This should take about 2-3 minutes per batch.

Drain Excess Oil:
- Use a slotted spoon to remove the risotto balls from the oil and place them on a plate lined with paper towels to drain any excess oil.

Serve:
- Serve the saffron and lemon risotto balls hot, perhaps with a side of marinara sauce for dipping.

These saffron and lemon risotto balls are a wonderful combination of creamy risotto with a crispy exterior. They make an elegant and flavorful appetizer for any occasion. Enjoy!

Roquefort and Walnut Stuffed Figs

Ingredients:

- Fresh figs (as many as needed)
- Roquefort cheese (or any blue cheese), crumbled
- Walnuts, halves or pieces
- Honey, for drizzling
- Fresh thyme leaves (optional, for garnish)

Instructions:

Preheat Oven:
- Preheat your oven to 350°F (175°C).

Prepare Figs:
- Wash and dry the fresh figs. Cut a small "X" at the top of each fig, being careful not to cut all the way through.

Stuff with Roquefort and Walnuts:
- Gently open each fig by pressing on the base, creating a little pocket. Fill the pocket with crumbled Roquefort cheese, and place a walnut half or piece on top.

Arrange on Baking Sheet:
- Place the stuffed figs on a baking sheet lined with parchment paper.

Bake:
- Bake in the preheated oven for about 10-12 minutes or until the cheese is melted, and the figs are softened.

Drizzle with Honey:
- Once out of the oven, drizzle honey over the stuffed figs for a touch of sweetness.

Garnish (Optional):
- Garnish with fresh thyme leaves for added flavor and a pop of color.

Serve:
- Arrange the Roquefort and walnut-stuffed figs on a serving platter and serve either warm or at room temperature.

These Roquefort and walnut-stuffed figs make an elegant and flavorful appetizer that's perfect for entertaining or special occasions. The combination of sweet figs, tangy Roquefort cheese, crunchy walnuts, and the drizzle of honey creates a harmonious and sophisticated flavor profile. Enjoy!

Basil Pesto Palmiers

Ingredients:

- 1 sheet puff pastry, thawed if frozen
- 1/2 cup basil pesto (store-bought or homemade)
- 1/4 cup grated Parmesan cheese
- 1 egg, beaten (for egg wash)
- Salt and black pepper to taste (optional)
- Fresh basil leaves for garnish (optional)

Instructions:

Preheat Oven:
- Preheat your oven to 400°F (200°C).

Roll Out Puff Pastry:
- On a lightly floured surface, roll out the puff pastry sheet to smooth out any creases.

Spread Pesto:
- Spread a layer of basil pesto evenly over the entire surface of the puff pastry sheet.

Sprinkle with Parmesan:
- Sprinkle the grated Parmesan cheese over the pesto layer. Optionally, season with a pinch of salt and black pepper to taste.

Fold and Roll:
- Starting from one of the longer sides, carefully fold the pastry sheet inward towards the center, creating a log shape. Repeat from the opposite side until the two folds meet in the middle.

Chill (Optional):
- For easier slicing, you can chill the rolled puff pastry in the refrigerator for about 15-30 minutes.

Slice Palmiers:
- Using a sharp knife, slice the rolled puff pastry into 1/2-inch thick slices. You should get pinwheel-like shapes.

Arrange on Baking Sheet:
- Place the sliced palmiers on a baking sheet lined with parchment paper, spacing them apart.

Brush with Egg Wash:

- Brush the tops of the palmiers with the beaten egg to give them a golden color when baked.

Bake:
- Bake in the preheated oven for about 12-15 minutes or until the palmiers are puffed and golden brown.

Garnish (Optional):
- Optionally, garnish with fresh basil leaves for a pop of color and added freshness.

Serve:
- Allow the basil pesto palmiers to cool slightly before serving. They can be enjoyed warm or at room temperature.

These basil pesto palmiers make a flavorful and impressive appetizer that's perfect for parties, gatherings, or as a snack. The combination of basil pesto and Parmesan in flaky puff pastry creates a delicious and elegant treat. Enjoy!

Roasted Beet and Whipped Goat Cheese Crostini

Ingredients:

- French baguette, thinly sliced
- 2 medium-sized beets, roasted and peeled
- 4 ounces goat cheese, softened
- 2 tablespoons cream cheese, softened
- 1 tablespoon honey
- Fresh thyme leaves for garnish
- Salt and black pepper to taste
- Olive oil for drizzling

Instructions:

For Roasted Beets:

Preheat Oven:
- Preheat your oven to 400°F (200°C).

Roast Beets:
- Wash and trim the beets. Wrap each beet in aluminum foil and place them on a baking sheet. Roast in the preheated oven for about 45-60 minutes or until the beets are tender. Allow them to cool before peeling.

Peel and Dice Beets:
- Once cooled, peel the roasted beets and dice them into small, bite-sized pieces.

For Whipped Goat Cheese:

Whip Goat Cheese:
- In a bowl, combine softened goat cheese, cream cheese, honey, salt, and black pepper. Use a hand mixer or whisk to whip the mixture until smooth and fluffy.

Assemble Crostini:
- Toast the thinly sliced baguette rounds in the oven or on a grill until they are lightly golden.
- Spread a generous layer of the whipped goat cheese mixture onto each toasted baguette slice.
- Top each crostini with diced roasted beets.

Garnish and Drizzle:
- Drizzle a small amount of honey over each crostini.
- Garnish with fresh thyme leaves for added flavor and a pop of color.

Serve:
- Arrange the roasted beet and whipped goat cheese crostini on a serving platter and serve immediately.

These crostini are not only visually appealing but also a delightful combination of flavors and textures. The sweetness of the roasted beets, the creaminess of whipped goat cheese, and the hint of honey create a well-balanced and elegant appetizer. Enjoy!

Chicken Liver Pate on Baguette Slices

Ingredients:

For Chicken Liver Pâté:

- 1 pound chicken livers, trimmed
- 1 small onion, finely chopped
- 2 cloves garlic, minced
- 1/2 cup unsalted butter
- 1/4 cup brandy or cognac
- 1 teaspoon fresh thyme leaves
- Salt and black pepper to taste
- 1/2 cup heavy cream

For Baguette Slices:

- 1 French baguette, sliced
- Olive oil for brushing
- Fresh parsley or chives for garnish (optional)

Instructions:

For Chicken Liver Pâté:

Clean and Trim Chicken Livers:
- Rinse the chicken livers under cold water and pat them dry with paper towels. Trim any excess fat or connective tissue.

Sauté Onions and Garlic:
- In a skillet over medium heat, melt 2 tablespoons of butter. Add finely chopped onions and minced garlic. Sauté until the onions are soft and translucent.

Cook Chicken Livers:
- Increase the heat to medium-high and add the chicken livers to the skillet. Cook for about 3-4 minutes on each side or until they are browned on the outside but still slightly pink in the center.

Deglaze with Brandy:

- Pour brandy or cognac into the skillet to deglaze the pan, scraping up any browned bits. Let it simmer for a minute to reduce slightly.

Add Thyme and Seasoning:
- Stir in fresh thyme leaves, salt, and black pepper to taste. Cook for an additional 1-2 minutes.

Blend into Smooth Pâté:
- Transfer the contents of the skillet to a food processor. Add the remaining butter and heavy cream. Blend until the mixture is smooth and creamy.

Strain (Optional):
- For an extra smooth texture, you can strain the pâté through a fine-mesh sieve to remove any coarser bits.

Chill:
- Transfer the chicken liver pâté to a bowl or ramekin. Cover and refrigerate for at least 2 hours to allow the flavors to meld.

For Baguette Slices:

Slice Baguette:
- Preheat your oven or a grill. Slice the French baguette into thin rounds.

Brush with Olive Oil:
- Brush each baguette slice with olive oil on both sides.

Toast:
- Toast the baguette slices in the oven or on the grill until they are golden brown and crisp.

Assembly:

Spread Pâté:
- Once the baguette slices are ready, spread a generous amount of the chilled chicken liver pâté onto each slice.

Garnish (Optional):
- Garnish with fresh parsley or chives for a touch of freshness.

Serve:
- Arrange the chicken liver pâté-topped baguette slices on a serving platter and serve immediately.

This chicken liver pâté on baguette slices is a luxurious and savory appetizer that's perfect for entertaining. The creamy pâté pairs wonderfully with the crunchy baguette, creating a combination of textures and flavors that's sure to delight your guests. Enjoy!

Sushi-grade Tuna Nachos

Ingredients:

For the Tuna:

- 1/2 pound sushi-grade tuna, diced
- 2 tablespoons soy sauce
- 1 tablespoon sesame oil
- 1 tablespoon rice vinegar
- 1 teaspoon honey
- 1 teaspoon ginger, minced
- 1 teaspoon sesame seeds
- 1 green onion, finely chopped

For the Nachos:

- Wonton wrappers or tortilla chips
- 1 avocado, diced
- 1/2 cup cucumber, diced
- 1/4 cup radishes, thinly sliced
- 1/4 cup red onion, finely chopped
- Fresh cilantro leaves for garnish
- Sriracha mayo (1/4 cup mayonnaise mixed with 1-2 tablespoons Sriracha sauce)

Instructions:

For the Tuna:

    Prepare Tuna Marinade:
- In a bowl, whisk together soy sauce, sesame oil, rice vinegar, honey, minced ginger, and sesame seeds.

    Marinate Tuna:
- Add the diced sushi-grade tuna to the marinade. Toss to coat evenly. Let it marinate in the refrigerator for at least 15-30 minutes.

    Assemble Tuna Mix:

- After marinating, drain any excess liquid from the tuna. Add finely chopped green onion and mix well.

For the Nachos:

Prepare Wonton Wrappers (Optional):
- If using wonton wrappers, cut them into triangles and deep-fry or bake until golden and crispy. If using tortilla chips, skip this step.

Assemble Nachos:
- Arrange the crispy wonton triangles or tortilla chips on a serving platter.

Add Tuna Mix:
- Spoon the marinated tuna mixture over the wonton triangles or chips.

Top with Fresh Ingredients:
- Scatter diced avocado, cucumber, thinly sliced radishes, and finely chopped red onion over the tuna.

Drizzle Sriracha Mayo:
- Drizzle the Sriracha mayo over the nachos for added flavor and a touch of heat.

Garnish:
- Garnish the sushi-grade tuna nachos with fresh cilantro leaves.

Serve Immediately:
- Serve the nachos immediately, ensuring they are enjoyed while the wonton or chips are still crispy and the tuna is fresh.

These sushi-grade tuna nachos offer a delightful fusion of Japanese and Mexican flavors. The combination of fresh tuna, vibrant vegetables, and a hint of spice from the Sriracha mayo creates a unique and satisfying appetizer. Enjoy!

Raspberry and Brie Puff Pastry Pinwheels

Ingredients:

- 1 sheet puff pastry, thawed if frozen
- 1/2 cup raspberry jam
- 6 ounces Brie cheese, rind removed and sliced
- 1 egg (for egg wash)
- Fresh thyme leaves for garnish (optional)
- Powdered sugar for dusting (optional)

Instructions:

Preheat Oven:
- Preheat your oven to 400°F (200°C).

Roll Out Puff Pastry:
- On a lightly floured surface, roll out the puff pastry sheet to smooth out any creases.

Spread Raspberry Jam:
- Spread a layer of raspberry jam evenly over the entire surface of the puff pastry.

Layer Brie Slices:
- Place the slices of Brie cheese over the raspberry jam, covering the entire surface.

Roll Puff Pastry:
- Starting from one of the longer sides, carefully roll the puff pastry into a log or cylinder shape. Roll it tightly but gently.

Chill (Optional):
- For easier slicing, you can chill the rolled puff pastry in the refrigerator for about 15-30 minutes.

Slice into Pinwheels:
- Using a sharp knife, slice the rolled puff pastry into 1/2-inch thick pinwheels.

Arrange on Baking Sheet:
- Place the pinwheels on a baking sheet lined with parchment paper, spacing them apart.

Brush with Egg Wash:

- Beat the egg and brush it over the tops of the pinwheels. This will give them a golden color when baked.

Bake:
- Bake in the preheated oven for about 15-18 minutes or until the pinwheels are puffed and golden.

Garnish (Optional):
- Optionally, garnish the Raspberry and Brie puff pastry pinwheels with fresh thyme leaves for added flavor.

Dust with Powdered Sugar (Optional):
- If desired, dust the pinwheels with powdered sugar just before serving for a touch of sweetness.

Serve:
- Arrange the pinwheels on a serving platter and serve them warm.

These Raspberry and Brie puff pastry pinwheels make a delicious and visually appealing appetizer, perfect for parties, brunches, or any special occasion. The combination of sweet raspberry jam and creamy Brie cheese wrapped in flaky puff pastry creates a delightful flavor profile. Enjoy!

Marinated Artichoke Hearts with Parmesan

Ingredients:

- 1 can (about 14 ounces) marinated artichoke hearts, drained
- 2 tablespoons extra-virgin olive oil
- 2 tablespoons balsamic vinegar
- 1 clove garlic, minced
- 1/4 cup freshly grated Parmesan cheese
- Salt and black pepper to taste
- Fresh parsley for garnish (optional)

Instructions:

Prepare Artichoke Hearts:
- Drain the marinated artichoke hearts and pat them dry with a paper towel.

Make Marinade:
- In a bowl, whisk together the extra-virgin olive oil, balsamic vinegar, minced garlic, and a pinch of salt and black pepper.

Marinate Artichoke Hearts:
- Place the drained artichoke hearts in the marinade, ensuring they are well-coated. Allow them to marinate for at least 30 minutes to let the flavors infuse.

Grate Parmesan:
- Grate fresh Parmesan cheese. You can adjust the quantity based on your preference.

Assemble:
- Arrange the marinated artichoke hearts on a serving platter. Drizzle any remaining marinade over the top.

Sprinkle with Parmesan:
- Sprinkle the grated Parmesan cheese over the artichoke hearts.

Garnish (Optional):
- Garnish with fresh parsley for a pop of color and added freshness.

Serve:
- Serve the marinated artichoke hearts with Parmesan at room temperature as an appetizer. You can also provide toothpicks or small forks for easy serving.

These marinated artichoke hearts with Parmesan are not only delicious but also quick to prepare. The combination of the tangy marinade, the tender artichoke hearts, and the savory Parmesan creates a flavorful and satisfying appetizer. Enjoy!

Mini Crab Cakes with Remoulade Sauce

Ingredients:

For the Crab Cakes:

- 1 pound lump crab meat, picked over for shells
- 1/3 cup mayonnaise
- 1 large egg, beaten
- 1 tablespoon Dijon mustard
- 1 tablespoon Worcestershire sauce
- 1 teaspoon Old Bay seasoning
- 1/2 teaspoon salt
- 1/4 teaspoon black pepper
- 1 cup breadcrumbs, divided
- 2 tablespoons unsalted butter, for cooking

For the Remoulade Sauce:

- 1/2 cup mayonnaise
- 2 tablespoons Dijon mustard
- 1 tablespoon capers, chopped
- 1 tablespoon cornichons or pickles, finely chopped
- 1 tablespoon fresh parsley, finely chopped
- 1 teaspoon hot sauce (adjust to taste)
- 1 teaspoon lemon juice
- Salt and pepper to taste

Instructions:

For the Crab Cakes:

Prepare Crab Mixture:
- In a large bowl, combine the lump crab meat, mayonnaise, beaten egg, Dijon mustard, Worcestershire sauce, Old Bay seasoning, salt, and black pepper. Gently fold the ingredients together to avoid breaking up the crab meat.

Add Breadcrumbs:
- Gradually add 1/2 cup of breadcrumbs to the crab mixture and gently combine. If the mixture seems too wet, add more breadcrumbs until it holds together.

Form Mini Crab Cakes:
- Shape the crab mixture into small, bite-sized crab cakes, about 1 to 1.5 inches in diameter.

Coat with Breadcrumbs:
- Coat each crab cake with the remaining breadcrumbs, pressing gently to adhere.

Pan-Fry Crab Cakes:
- In a large skillet, melt butter over medium heat. Cook the mini crab cakes for about 2-3 minutes per side or until golden brown and cooked through.

For the Remoulade Sauce:

Mix Ingredients:
- In a bowl, whisk together mayonnaise, Dijon mustard, chopped capers, chopped cornichons or pickles, fresh parsley, hot sauce, lemon juice, salt, and pepper.

Chill Sauce:
- Refrigerate the remoulade sauce for at least 30 minutes to allow the flavors to meld.

Serve:

- Arrange the mini crab cakes on a serving platter with a bowl of remoulade sauce on the side for dipping.

These mini crab cakes with remoulade sauce are sure to be a hit at your next gathering. The combination of the crispy exterior and the tender, flavorful crab interior, paired with the tangy remoulade sauce, creates a delightful appetizer. Enjoy!

Blue Cheese and Walnut-Stuffed Dates

Ingredients:

- Medjool dates (as many as needed)
- Blue cheese (Roquefort, Gorgonzola, or your favorite blue cheese), crumbled
- Walnut halves

Instructions:

Prepare Dates:
- Using a sharp knife, make a lengthwise slit in each date, being careful not to cut all the way through. Gently open the date to remove the pit.

Stuff with Blue Cheese:
- Take a small amount of crumbled blue cheese (about a teaspoon) and stuff it into the cavity of each date.

Insert Walnut Halves:
- Place a walnut half on top of the blue cheese, pressing it slightly into the opening of the date.

Arrange on a Platter:
- Arrange the stuffed dates on a serving platter. You can stand them upright or lay them flat, depending on your preference.

Serve:
- Serve the blue cheese and walnut-stuffed dates at room temperature. They are ready to be enjoyed as a delicious and elegant appetizer.

These stuffed dates are a perfect blend of sweetness from the dates, creaminess from the blue cheese, and crunch from the walnuts. They make an excellent addition to cheese platters or appetizer spreads and are sure to impress your guests. Enjoy!

www.ingramcontent.com/pod-product-compliance
Lightning Source LLC
LaVergne TN
LVHW081606060526
838201LV00054B/2096